CLAUDIUS THE BEE

CLAUDIUS THE BEE

John F. Leeming

decorated by
Richard B. Ogle

Harrap London

First published 1936
by George G. Harrap & Co. Ltd
182 High Holborn, London WC1V 7AX

Reset and reprinted 1952

Reissued 1980

ISBN 0 245 53584 5

Printed and bound in Great Britain by
Redwood Burn Limited
Trowbridge & Esher

Contents

The characters in this story are not fictitious and reference is made to actual living persons.

The Song of Claudius

Arranged for the pianoforte by

VINCENT WAGTAIL, Honorary Bee

I

Before the Story starts

ALTHOUGH this is the story of Claudius the Bee, Mr Tawney plays such an important part that it seems only fair to mention him first.

Mr Tawney lived in the country. His house was not a large one, polite people called it 'cosy.' This was one of the ways Mr Tawney had of deciding if they were polite, for there were some people who called it a 'pokey hole.'

Around the house there was a large garden. Long stretches of turf so neat and smooth that they looked like strips of green carpet some giant had unrolled. Great masses of flowers in wide borders, flowers not 'bedded out' so that they stood in rows like soldiers, but big clumps, one colour mingling with another. There were also some large trees in the garden, old oak-trees with trunks big enough for a small person to live inside. And then, of course, there was the pool, a nice stretch of water very useful for sailing model boats upon; although here, in summer, the water-lilies were inclined to grow rather too much and leave only the smallest channels down which a ship might sail.

There were all sorts of animals about this garden,

and sometimes Mr Tawney was kept quite busy helping these. For he discovered that many animals had a way of doing silly things that often got them into serious danger. The Hedgehogs, for instance. If the gardener ever dug a trench, as he sometimes did when there were field-drains to be put in, some Hedgehog was sure to fall into the trench during the night. Mr Tawney made it a custom to go round any trench that might be dug and see if an unhappy animal was lying at the bottom. A few hours in a warm shed, with a little bread-and-milk and some raw meat, Mr Tawney found, usually enabled such a Hedgehog to recover.

Then there were the Squirrels, Wild Ducks, Owls, Rabbits, and even the Fish. All these did silly things at times, and Mr Tawney became quite an expert at nursing them back to health. He had a book, *The Balance of Nature*, which told just exactly what each animal or bird liked best to eat.

Now one day he came into his house and found a Bee dying on the window-sill. It was one of those big furry Bees; not the thin, sleek kind that cluster in man-made hives, but a wild Bumble-Bee that lives in a hole in a bank. And when Mr Tawney found it, it seemed very unlikely that this particular Bee would ever fly in the sunlight again.

Apparently, on its way to gather honey, this Bee had noticed an open window in Mr Tawney's house, and, having that inquisitive nature which is so common among the Bee people, had popped inside to have a look round. Some one had come into the room and, not noticing the Bee, had closed the window. Then they had gone out of the room and closed the door.

At first the Bumble-Bee had not realized that he was trapped. He buzzed across the panes, seeking the way out into the sunlight, puzzled that such a heavy and obviously solid thing as this window was could have been moved. Then he flew about the room looking for some other way of escape, but always he came back to the light of the window.

After a time he became frightened, and buzzed frantically backward and forward. It was cold in this room, and Bees cannot stand cold—at least, not if they are using their strength in panic-stricken dashes against a window-pane. Soon his terrified struggles became less and less, and he began to feel very ill indeed.

In the end he sank down by the side of the glass, too worn-out to fight any longer. This was the end, he knew; already he felt drowsy, in a little while he would be too numb to move, then . . . Outside was the warm sunshine, the precious honey in the flowers. . . .

Mr Tawney found him, and opened the window at once; but the Bumble-Bee was too exhausted to fly out, too weary to get to the warmth and to the honey that would save his life.

For a few minutes Mr Tawney watched him; then, as he saw the Bee could not move but lay stretched out, dazed and dying, he realized that if anything was to be done it would be he who would have to do it.

He ran quickly from the room and up into his bedroom. Here there was a drawer in which he kept

an assortment of things: boxes, cards, a night-light glass, pencils, string, a note-book, a penknife, a fountain-pen, and a dozen other useful articles. Among these he found a match-box and some cotton-wool. He opened the match-box, dropped the top part back into the drawer, and into the bottom of the box he stuffed some of the cotton-wool; in this way making a tiny bed, a little square box with a soft, white mattress of wool inside it.

Hurrying downstairs again, Mr Tawney placed the little box by the open window, just where the glass protected it from the summer breeze, but where it was in the open sunlight. Then, slipping a sheet of paper gently under the dying Bee, he lifted it carefully into the tiny bed.

"If you only rest there for a little while," said Mr Tawney, "you may pull round."

Once the Bee was safely in the sunlight Mr Tawney left him and went to the pantry, where the

jars of honey were stored. One of these jars was open. He took a teaspoon from the basket and dipped it into the top of the honey; then, with just a smearing sticking to the spoon, he went back to the open window. Taking care not to touch the Bee, he dropped a spot or two of the honey on to the corner of the little box.

"If you can manage to eat some," he murmured, "it'll do you good. It's very strengthening, you know."

After which, feeling that he had done all that could be done, Mr Tawney strolled out into the garden.

Down at the pool the fish were jumping for flies. The growing circles on the surface of the water told Mr Tawney this. He sat down on the bank where the willow, as it hung over, offered some shade in the brilliant summer sunshine. It was very warm. Only the faint splash of a fish leaping at some fly, and occasionally the popping of a seed-pod in the gorse near by, broke the silence.

II

The Return of Oswego

THE warm sunlight poured down on to the box on which the Bee lay—soft, caressing sunlight that found its way even through the thick, woolly fur of the Bee and soothed his tired body with its gentle heat. Presently the Bee stirred.

After a while he rubbed one leg against another. Why, he could feel that, he noticed with surprise; his legs no longer seemed numb and lifeless, he could move them; for a moment he lay there, gently waving each one in turn. Yes, they all moved just as they had always done. Perhaps he was not going to die after all?

For perhaps ten minutes he rested on the soft cotton-wool, contented to stay as he was, gradually recovering his strength. How good it seemed to feel a little better, almost worth being ill, to feel like this!

He was still too weak to fly, his wings hung limp and soft at his side, but if he waited . . . The faint scent of the honey Mr Tawney had placed at the end of the box reached him. With an effort he stood up, and then he crawled towards it.

Half an hour later he sat briskly cleaning his legs, smoothing his ruffled fur, paw over paw across his hairy head. He felt quite all right now—that honey had put new life into him. Comfy sort of place: that Tawney chap knew how to do himself well. How soft and warm the white wool seemed!

Still, no good staying any longer. They'd be worried at the Nest by now, probably sending search-parties out. Anyway, he'd have something to tell them when he did get back. Not many Bees could say they'd been trapped in a cold prison for hours and come through alive. He could picture the other Bees gathering round as he told his tale. . . . That thought stirred him to action.

"Oswego, my boy," he murmured to himself, "you'd better be on your way."

He stood up, flicked his wings a few times to test them, and a moment later was flying swiftly towards his home.

"Way for a worker"

2

On the rocky terrace at the mouth of the Nest a small crowd of Bees had gathered and were murmuring anxiously among themselves. From time to time one of the Guard Bees, one of the detachment on duty at the hive-entrance, would move along the fringe of the crowd, clearing a passage as some worker Bee arrived or departed.

"Gangway, please!" the Guard Bee would call. "Way for a worker. Plenty of room at the sides. Don't block the entrance, *if* you please."

The Captain of the Guards looked moodily out across the valley to where the tall delphinium spikes showed against the skyline. He hardly seemed to hear the frequent calls of his men on the terrace.

"I'm afraid it's all up with him," he said at last, turning to a Sergeant who stood behind. "That's the third search-party to come back in the last half-hour. They haven't seen a trace of him."

The Sergeant moved his curved sword, a thorn from a rose-stem, and nodded gloomily.

"Away more than three solid hours; no Bee living can last all that time away from 'is Nest. I remember in the second 'Eather Campaign—I was a young Bee at the time, sir, young and fit—full of 'ealth and strength——"

The Captain interrupted the reminiscence.

"Yes," he said, "I'm afraid there's no hope now. Claudius will be heart-broken."

"They do say, sir, as Claudius is that sad——" The Sergeant broke off hurriedly, stared for a moment across the valley, then suddenly waved his sword. "That's 'im!" he shouted excitedly. "Coming over them antirrhinums over there. It is, I tell you!"

The Captain sprang alertly to attention—stared out into the sunlight.

"You're right. Turn out the Guard. Clear a passage. Send a messenger to Claudius."

Raising one of his front paws in a rapid salute, the Sergeant jumped to obey orders. There was a stir among the crowd gathered on the terrace, and other Bees, warned by the noise, rushed from the Nest.

Thirty seconds later, as Oswego swooped down towards the entrance, he saw below him a mass of excited Bees covering the terrace. In vain the Guards tried to clear a space for him to land. Bees were swarming everywhere, newcomers tumbling

The Return of Oswego

one after another from the doorway of the Nest, pushing, even climbing over one another in their determination to see the arrival. It was with the greatest difficulty that, at last, Oswego found a tiny spot by the edge of the wall, and hung there until a dozen willing paws pulled him to safety.

The noise of his welcome was deafening. All the Bees were giving that shrill 'buzz' which signifies satisfaction and is equivalent to human cheering.

"Tell us what happened! Good old Oswego! How did you get back? Did the wasps attack you? Down with the wasps! What happened?"

At last the Captain and a few of the Guards

managed to reach him and to form a ring against the surging crowds.

"I hope you're all right, sir," yelled the Captain.

"I am not sure," replied Oswego. "Some of these people have been pulling out bits of my fur."

"Just for souvenirs, sir; a crowd wants a few souvenirs to take away," excused the Captain.

"Well, they ought to be more careful," Oswego muttered. "Kept pulling out hairs, and every time I turned round to catch them at it some one on the other side plucked at me. I'll be as bald as an onion."

Oswego complains of Souvenir-hunters

The Captain shook his head.

"Bees will be Bees, sir, and at a time like this, when they're so relieved to find you safe——"

"Be that as it may," said Oswego, "some of them were playing 'She loves me, she loves me not' with my fur, and I resent it strongly."

A young agile Bee wriggled his way forward and, pushing his head between the legs of the Guard, addressed Oswego.

"Excuse me, sir," he called. "I represent the journal *Hive and Honey*; if you would be good enough to favour me with an exclusive interview——"

At that moment a new sound seemed to swell the shouting, a sound that steadily grew louder and gradually overcame the frantic buzzing.

"Way for Claudius," it boomed. "Silence for Claudius. Claudius comes."

As if by magic, some order seemed to come upon the excited crowd. The struggling, pushing mass subsided, and when at the entrance of the Nest appeared a little cavalcade, the crowd stepped back, leaving a clear way: four Guard Bees with curved swords held upright in front of them; two Courtier Bees waving wands of grass; and then Claudius himself.

Oswego watched the procession winding slowly towards him, the cheering crowds closing in behind it, and, often as he had seen Claudius, it occurred to him once again what a fine Bee he was. For all his

age—he had seen more than four seasons in the Nest—he strode along firmly, briskly alert. Slightly larger than the Guards, his great width made him seem doubly imposing. His silky fur glistened in the sunlight, deep black fur relieved by broad bands of fawn.

Oswego remembered a comment made last summer when, flying by the heather, Claudius had rested for a moment near a lady.

"Goodness gracious!" the lady had cried. "Look, the father of all bees!"

At last the cavalcade reached Oswego. The Guard Bees divided and stepped backward; the two Courtier Bees took up their position on each side of Claudius, and Oswego found himself face to face with the master of the Nest.

"We have been very anxious about you," Claudius

began. "Every one felt sure something terrible had happened."

"And it did," said Oswego. "Indeed, I marvel that I am here at all. I have been like Jonah attacked by whales, like Daniel beset by lions, like——"

"That's all right," interrupted Claudius, and he placed his two front paws on the shoulders of Oswego. "Tell me, tell us all," he went on, in a kindly voice, "just what did really happen."

The young Bee who represented the journal *Hive and Honey* pushed himself forward.

"We ought to have a photograph of this," he said anxiously. "My News Editor will want one badly. 'Claudius congratulates prominent Bee on his escape from death. Terrifying experience. Exclusive story.'"

"You give 'ush," the Sergeant of the Guard corrected. "Why, when I was a young Bee in the second 'Eather Campaign . . ."

Claudius glanced round, and the murmurs died away.

"Now, Oswego," he said, "tell us just what happened."

And so Oswego began. He was a good story-teller, and he kept the Bees around him thrilled. He told how he found himself trapped in the cold room, how he struggled to find a way out, and how, gradually, his strength left him. He told how, when he was on the point of death, Mr Tawney had found him, told of the box with its soft bed of warm cotton-wool, of the life-saving honey. The crowd groaned with anxiety at the story of his struggles, howled with delight at the tale of his escape, cheered frantically as Mr Tawney's action became plain to them.

A Press Photographer

"It is truly wonderful," said Claudius.

"What surprised me," added Oswego, "was the strength of the man. Believe me or believe me not, he picked me up as if I were a feather. Now, I'm no light weight——"

"Ay, he's a fat 'un!" shouted some one in the crowd.

Oswego glared towards the speaker.

"I am *not* fat," he said; "far from it. I am well-proportioned, I am a well-developed Bee, yet he picked me up as if I weighed only a dram or so. The man must be as strong as a Tom-Tit."

The Sergeant of the Guard shook his head.

"When I was a young Bee," he began, "I was that strong, that hefty——"

Claudius, who had been standing silent, now turned and spoke to the crowd.

The Captain of the Guard

"You have heard a remarkable story," he boomed; "you have been told of this kindly man of great strength who has saved our friend; to him we owe much. I say that every Bee in this Nest should be grateful to this Mr Tawney."

"We are!" howled the crowd. "Bright sunshine and open flowers in plenty for Mr Tawney! The Bee people never forget!"

"Exactly," Claudius went on when the tumult subsided. "We never forget a kindness, and in this case I feel we should take some exceptional way of showing our gratitude. Bees, to the council hall! I call you all, every Bee in this Nest, to an assembly in the Great Hall, for I have a proposal to make, and, as is our custom, each Bee has the right to say 'aye' or 'nay.' I call the Free Bee people to council!"

The Sergeant of the Guard

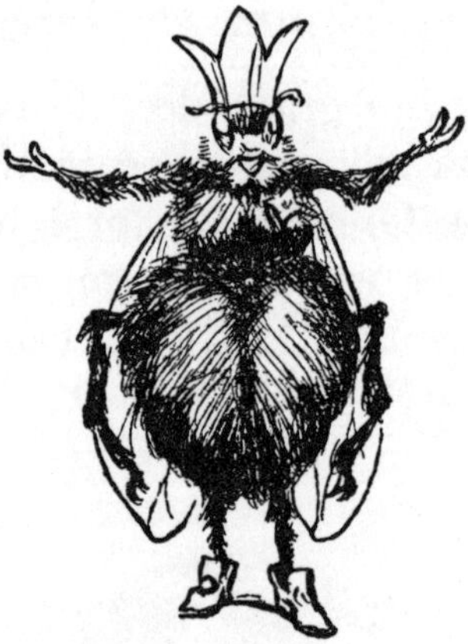

III

The Invitation to Tawney

CLAUDIUS had been speaking for some time, and when he paused the Bees crowded in the hall stirred uneasily. Except for a few Guard Bees, who remained on duty at the entrance, every inhabitant of the Nest was present. Packed wing to wing, they had listened in silence to the appeal Claudius had made.

"It is not one isolated act of kindness," Claudius went on; "you have heard of numerous helpful things this Mr Tawney has done for animals. Yet with these we have no concern; let the Blackbird folk squeak their own gratitude, let the Hedgehog people grunt their thanks; what they do is no concern of the Bee people. What does concern us is that one of our company has been saved from a terrible death; that we owe to this Mr Tawney a debt. Bees, let us pay this debt!"

There was silence for a few moments after Claudius stopped speaking and stepped back as a sign that he had finished; then at last a young Bee near the back raised his head and spoke.

"I should like to ask the speaker," he began, "how he would—er—introduce this Mr Tawney into the Nest? He is, I understand, a large man, of some ten years of age; now how could such a clumsy being get into our passages and halls?"

Some of the older Bees smiled, and an elderly Professor Bee immediately rose to reply.

"I may say that the point our young friend raises would cause little difficulty. We who devote our lives to research have long known of a process by which a living animal may be reduced in size. We have experimented with numerous creatures. My friend Professor Retort conducted various experiments, using fleas as his subject. I understand that, unfortunately, he caused some of these fleas to become so minute that the eye could not see them—but that is incidental. We can, if required, reduce this Mr Tawney to a height of approximately one inch. The process is simple: a preparation of the juices of certain flowers."

"Yes; but how about getting him back to his proper size again?" some one objected. "If you make him small enough to come into our Nest and then can't get him back again you'll have that Mother of his making trouble. Real trouble."

The Professor Bee smiled indulgently.

"There is not the slightest risk of failure in the process," he said confidently. "The preparation which causes reduction is made by distilling the juice of certain tiny flowers—the toadflax, the soapwort, the bugloss, the fleabane—and mixing them together. To bring the subject back to his normal size again we use the same juices but mix them together the opposite way round, starting with the fleabane and finishing with the toadflax. The first order of mixing reduces, the second order increases: I trust I have made myself clear?"

The Professor bowed right and left, and then sank down into the crowd again.

"But how would you talk to him?" some one called out.

Claudius himself stepped forward.

"I hope," he said severely, "that we are not so ignorant here that we cannot speak Human if it is

required of us. Every Bee is taught Human at school, and I trust our education is not so poor that we have all forgotten this teaching."

The Bees murmured among themselves.

"Of course. Why, I speak Human like a native," whispered one.

"I find it most amusing to listen to Human talk," said another. "I often go and hear that Henry Hall humming and banging. A bit loud, perhaps, but pleasant from a distance."

"My greatest pleasure," droned a large Bee with almost golden fur, "is to listen to that dear Human. I must admit I fly away when he commences to say 'Before the news there are three SOS's,' but often I find him quite entertaining."

At this moment a large black Bee who had been standing at the back of the hall raised himself up. He was a powerful creature, even coarse in his strength, and on his unpleasant face was a sneering look, as if he would delight in another's discomfort.

"Bees," he began, "we have heard a proposal that a human being should be invited to visit us; that he should be given great honours among us; that he should be made an Honorary Bee. Friends, it ill

becomes me, one of the humblest of Bees, to question the ways of the great Claudius, but just why is this thing—this bringing of a stranger into our Nest—to be done? Friends, because one of our number, the Bee Oswego, has come back with some vague

story of a human being who did him some supposed kindness. What proof have we that what this Bee Oswego tells us has really ever happened? I suggest that perhaps, heated by the sun, overfed with nectar

from the flowers, he dreamt——"

"Am I to understand that you mean I made it all up?" demanded Oswego, springing forward.

The black Bee shrugged his shoulders.

"Well, what proof have you?" he sneered. "And if it did happen, is your life so valuable that the whole Nest must be inconvenienced with strangers?"

"I can't bear strangers," said one middle-aged Bee. "Can't abide 'em. Never could."

"No strangers in the Nest," shouted three or four rough-looking Bees who were standing near the back of the hall.

Claudius once more stepped forward.

"Bees," he cried, "it is for you to decide. You are a free people. You are met here together in the council hall. Shall we pay our debt to this Tawney? Shall he be made an Honorary Bee and invited to visit the Nest? You have heard. Judge then, and say 'aye' or 'nay.'"

There was a long pause, and then an elderly Bee with yellow whiskers stepped forward.

"I'm an old Bee," he said fiercely, "who has served the Nest in the Guards for more seasons than I care to remember. I have a better right to speak than anyone else. If we owe this feller Tawney anything, why, confound it! let us pay him. Let him come here, and I will be the first to shake him by the paw. I am an old Guard, and I speak plain Saxon Bee talk. Let him come!"

"I think it would be just *too* thrilling," cooed a dainty Bee, whose fur was carefully smoothed and brushed. "Just *too* thrilling."

There was a sudden movement in the crowd. The Bees had considered; they had made up their minds.

"Bring him here," they shouted. "Let him visit us. Let us thank Tawney ourselves."

"Free people, you say 'aye'?" asked Claudius.

"We do!" they howled. "We say 'aye'!"

Claudius raised a paw for silence.

"I will arrange for three members of the Nest to go at once and find this Tawney," he boomed. "They shall invite him on our behalf. Soon we should have his answer."

As the crowd prepared to depart, the elderly Bee with yellow whiskers sprang forward.

"Bees," he shouted, "let us sing the song we all know so well, the song of Claudius."

There was a shout of approval, and then the Bees burst into song, each one beating time upon the ground with his front paws!

> "O Claudius the Bee! O Claudius the Bee!
> Oh, what a pretty sight it is
> To see him wave his wings and fizz.
> O Claudius the Bee!" [1]

"So that's all settled," murmured Oswego, as the crowd began to depart.

"Yes," said Claudius thoughtfully; "but we must keep an eye on Black Michael. Some of the rougher Bees support him, and unless I am mistaken, Black Michael means to make trouble. Bad trouble."

[1] The music of the song *Claudius the Bee* will be found in the front of this book.

2

Down by the pool the fish were jumping for flies. The faint 'plop' as the fish leapt from the water could be heard occasionally. Even in the shade of the willow it was very warm; and the air was so still that the scent of the flowers away in the border at the top of the hill drifted slowly downward across the pool.

Mr Tawney realized that he had been dozing. A Bee seemed to be buzzing uncomfortably close to his head, to be hovering within an inch or so of his ear; then, as he raised his hand to drive it away, Mr Tawney saw it was not one Bee, but three. Three Bees close together, just by his ear.

"I trust we have not disturbed you," came a tiny voice. "Nothing is farther from our intention. We are—if I may say so—upon an errand of good will."

Mr Tawney sat quite still, he knew that he must be sleeping. Probably there were not any Bees there at

all. Bees could not talk, and yet . . . The buzzing became louder.

"If you will forgive us," came the voice, "we propose to settle upon your ear. Pray do not be alarmed for our safety, there is plenty of space for all three of us, and even a few hairs for us to cling to. On your ear we can discuss our business with you in comfort."

"You're tickling frightfully," cried Mr Tawney a moment later. "Ow! You're tickling."

"Indeed? We must apologize, we must indeed," said the Bee. "Perhaps if you were to lay your head down on the bank and we were to alight just by your ear upon the grass it would be better?"

"Oh yes," said Mr Tawney; "anything you like, only stop tickling."

The Bees sped into the air, and when he laid his head down upon the grass they settled down beside him.

"Allow me to introduce this deputation," said one of the Bees. "This"— he pointed with his paw to the largest of the party— "this is Colonel Mainsting, a warrior of considerable renown."

Colonel Mainsting

The Bee indicated raised his paw sharply in salute and then stood twisting his yellow whiskers, with a fierce expression on his face.

"This," the Bee went on, "is Oswego, one of our prominent and—if I may say it—one of the most popular members of the Nest."

"I may claim to have met you before, sir," said Oswego.

"May you—er—have you?" replied the bewildered Mr Tawney. "Well, your face does seem familiar."

"I myself," the Bee that had first spoken continued, "I am Professor Goatsbeard-Bugloss."

"I'm very pleased to meet you," Mr Tawney said; then added hastily, as he caught a look of annoyance on Colonel Mainsting's face: "Meet you all, I mean."

"And now let us explain our mission," said the Bee. "Let us explain why we have approached you in this manner. Let me explain our proposal."

Mr Tawney listened in amazement as the Professor continued. For perhaps five minutes he listened to him as he droned on. At last he managed to speak.

"It would be wonderful to see inside a hive."

"Nest," the Professor corrected. "Nest, not hive. Hives are the homes of—may I say—tame Bees, the tribes who live in wooden structures and gather their honey for the use of man. We are the Free Bee People. To use our official name—the

Bombus family. The Bumble people are dependent upon none. We live in a dwelling like an underground town inside a mountain. A mountain you would call a bank. It is an impressive and interesting city. You would see the Great Hall, the council hall, numerous corridors, and so on."

"And we should have a great banquet to celebrate your visit," put in Oswego.

"You would also see the Guards," Colonel Mainsting intervened. "The Guards, sir, who night and day protect the Nest and make it safe for decent Bees to go about their business. The Guards who keep the rascally Wasps in their place."

"I should simply love it!" said Mr Tawney.

"Then that's settled," Oswego chuckled.

"When can I come?" Mr Tawney asked.

The Professor rubbed his front paws one against the other.

"We suggest now. At once," he replied.

Mr Tawney thought it over for a moment.

"I've had tea," he said slowly. "I shan't be wanted for another two hours. Yes, let's go."

"The Nest is prepared," said the Professor, beginning to unfold his wings. "The people are waiting to receive you. Now if I were to fly back to arrange the little matter of the reducing juice, while my good friends here guide you to the Nest. . . ."

"I could fly slowly in front of him," offered Oswego; "he could follow me, walking."

"A soldier's place is in front," interrupted the Colonel. "You want an escort ready and able to deal with any rascally Wasp that might attack. You, Oswego, may fly on my flank."

The Professor Bee had his wings stretched ready for flight.

"Well, I'll leave you two to bring him to the Nest. I'll be off now to see the juice is ready when he arrives." Then, remembering an afternoon when he had popped inside the window of a cinema, he added: "I'll be seeing you."

Mr Tawney rose to his feet.

"This way, sir," said Oswego.

"Forward!" bellowed the Colonel.

"I'll follow you," said Mr Tawney.

IV

The Professor makes a Mistake

THE excitement was terrific.

Around the entrance the Bees had gathered in a solid crowd, a crowd so tightly packed together that they looked like a carpet of brown wool. It was with the greatest difficulty that the Guards kept a passage clear between the people.

"Pushing an' pulling," said a Sergeant of the Guard. "If I've 'ad my toes trod on once I've 'ad 'em trod on twenty times. Suffer with corns I do."

"We want some more Guards to 'elp us," one of the sentries complained.

"Well, you can't 'ave 'em," said the Sergeant. "'Cos why? 'Cos every single Guard is 'ere already." He turned and marched along the line of sentries. "Stand back, there, *if* you please!" he called. "Back just another inch, please!"

Near the edge of the cliffs, in a small space the Guards had managed to clear, stood Claudius. He was surrounded by ten or twelve Courtier Bees, whose well-brushed golden fur glistened in the sunlight and made a splendid contrast with the deep brown fur on their heads.

"It is a great day for the Nest," Claudius commented. "You are sure everything is prepared?"

"Everything," the Chief Courtier assured him. "The band is assembled in the Great Hall; the Waiter Bees are ready to serve the banquet. Nothing has been forgotten."

"He should be here any moment now," Claudius said. "Yes, any moment."

As he spoke, a little party of Bees, headed by Professor Goatsbeard-Bugloss, appeared at the entrance of the Nest and made their way between the line of sentries. They were carrying between them a round bowl, which Claudius recognized as the top or cap of an acorn, and, as they bore it carefully along, its liquid contents sparkled invitingly.

"I suppose that is the reducing juice," said Claudius. "Are you sure there is enough of it?"

The Professor and his party paused.

"Certainly, certainly; ample, if I may say so; this is an exceptionally large dose," the Professor replied.

"Well, remember he is a large Human; we don't want him sticking in the entrance, or anything like that."

Before the Professor could answer there came a sudden howl from the waiting crowds. A tremendous shout:

"There he is! By the yew hedge! There's Oswego and the Colonel in front!"

The Professor, realizing it was impossible to make himself heard, signed to his party to continue on their way.

"Careful with that acorn cup!" he yelled frantically. "Do not spill any; use great care."

A few moments later Mr Tawney stood beside the Nest. He towered far above the excited Bees, like some tall building above people in the street below. Like some bird flying round a chimney-stack, Oswego hovered near Mr Tawney's ear.

"Now, sir," called Oswego, "below you is the Nest; there are the people gathered to greet you. I see Claudius himself waiting near the entrance."

"It's very good of him," said Mr Tawney nervously.

"Here is our friend Professor Bugloss and his assistants. One sip of his mixture, and you will become a proper size."

"Be so good," said the Professor, as his struggling assistants brought the acorn-cup level with Mr

Tawney's face; "be so good as to drink the contents of this bowl."

Mr Tawney hesitated.

"Is it nasty?" he questioned. "I once had some medicine, a tonic it was——"

The Professor waved his doubts aside.

"No flavour at all; well, hardly any," he said.

"You're sure you can get me back again to my right size? I mean after I've been in the hive——"

"Nest, sir!" roared Colonel Mainsting. "Confound it! Nest!"

"There is not the slightest doubt," the Professor said. "We can expand you, if I may say so, as easily as a piece of elastic. Larger or smaller as required."

Mr Tawney thought how interesting it would be to see inside a Bees' Nest, to walk about the corridors, to see their rooms, to see their stocks of honey. He held out his hand.

"Put the bowl on his hand," the Professor shouted to his assistants. "Careful, now; gently. Ah, that's right. Now, sir, be so good as to drink the contents."

Mr Tawney lifted the tiny cup to his lips, paused for a second, then licked the spot of liquid down.

Sweet; yes, sweet; rather like honey, he thought; no, not exactly like honey, more as if he had chewed the petals of a flower. He felt all right, no different at all.

"Does it take long to work?" he asked.

The Professor considered the question.

"I have never made the experiment before on a human being, so I cannot forecast the result precisely, but I should estimate that a change will commence within a few seconds. Once the change commences, the decrease in size will be very rapid."

As he spoke, Mr Tawney suddenly felt his clothes beginning to be heavier. His sleeves began to drop over his hands, and glancing down he saw his trousers were wrinkled, collapsing into folds. Suddenly, his collar pushed over his head and he found himself staring up through it at the sky, like a man looking up a chimney. He realized that, without his body to support them, his clothes were collapsing, falling into a heap near the entrance of the Nest. He seemed to be struggling in a cave, a huge cave formed by the soft cloth surrounding him.

The Professor's excited cries came through to Mr Tawney:

"A slight misjudgment. I entirely forgot that

the juice would have no effect upon the garments. The juice did not touch the garments and so——"

"Confound it!" howled the Colonel. "This is a nice reception for an honoured guest!"

In the dark cave formed by his clothes Mr Tawney pushed and struggled. Like some one beneath the blankets of a gigantic bed, he wriggled to find a way out. Over to one side, away beyond a hill of cloth, he saw a glimmer of light and, climbing quickly, came upon a tunnel, a wide tube three or four times his own height. He ran swiftly down the tunnel towards where the broad daylight showed, and as he did so it occurred to him that he was hurrying down his own sleeve.

Outside he could hear the shouting of the Bees; the wailing of the dismayed Professor:

"A most unfortunate occurrence. Entirely unexpected. Unforeseen . . ."

And the bellowing of the Colonel:

"You ought to be shot, sir; put before a marching regiment!"

And the cries of the confused Oswego:

"Can no one do anything? Why doesn't some one do something?"

A moment later Mr Tawney reached the end of the sleeve and popped out into the sunlight.

"I'm all right," he called. "Here I am. If some one would only get me a piece of cloth or something. It's cold like this."

There was a rush towards him.

"A thousand apologies!" cried the Professor. "One does not foresee these little points, one is apt to be carried away by enthusiasm. A most regrettable occurrence."

"Why doesn't some one bring a piece of cloth?" demanded Oswego—"some wool, a sheet of fur, anything. The man will catch his death of cold."

The Colonel turned on him angrily:

"Confound it, sir, do you think I'm a cloakroom, or what? Do you think I carry spare coats of fur around with me?"

Claudius, who had been watching the scene in silence, now signed to two of the Courtier Bees.

"That banner," he ordered. "Tear it down and take it to him. It will at least cover him until we can get a robe."

The Courtier Bees sprang for the banner, a strip of cloth with the words "Welcome to Tawney" printed upon it, which stretched between two poles at the entrance of the Nest. In an instant they had it down and, roughly folding it, flew rapidly away towards Tawney and the heap of clothes.

"If you will be so good as to wrap this round you," urged the Professor.

Mr Tawney draped the banner over his shoulders.

"It's rather large, I may trip over the ends," he said; "but perhaps I can manage."

"A disgrace to the Nest!" stormed the Colonel. "An honoured guest, and we dress him up like a—like I don't know what!"

"Like a scarecrow," suggested Oswego.

"When I want suggestions from you, sir," the Colonel said fiercely, "I'll ask for them. Until I do so, keep silent. Calling our guest a scarecrow! Why, confound it, sir, in the Guards we shoot Bees for less than that."

"I didn't mean——"

"Silence!" roared the Colonel. "Mr Tawney, sir, accept my apologies for these numbskulls. If I had them in my regiment, I'd know how to deal with them. Muddling boneheads, without manners or sense!"

"I'm really all right," Tawney said. "Really, I am. This banner is quite warm."

Oswego looked round anxiously to where Claudius waited among the clamouring crowds.

"If you feel you could walk this way?" he suggested.

"I feel fine," said Tawney pleasantly. "I can walk anywhere you want."

"Then this way, if you please."

Tawney stepped forward, the two Courtier Bees slipped behind him, and the Professor and his assistants, as if ashamed of their error, took their places at the back of them. Oswego put himself at Tawney's side. The Colonel pranced to the front.

"Ready?" he shouted; "then forward to the Nest!"

2

Claudius had finished his speech of welcome; the Guards had waved their rose-thorn swords in a general salute; and the crowds had buzzed their cheers until they stopped from sheer tiredness.

"You can see how pleased, how proud, the people are to have you here," said Claudius. "We Bee people never forget a kindness, and in your case it has not been just one act of kindness, but many seasons of helpful acts. We will obtain some proper clothes for you and then, if you are ready, we can proceed with our programme."

"Anything you say," murmured Tawney. "It's most interesting."

And interesting he really found it.

Meeting the Bees close to, standing beside them, his shoulders hardly reaching the top of Claudius's head, he was amazed to see how many things there were about a Bee that he had never noticed before. Their slender wings, so light and powerful, so suggestive of effortless flight. Their delicate paws, jointed like his own knees and elbows. Their glistening fur, so soft and woolly that it made them look like Teddy Bears—living, friendly Teddy Bears ready for a romp. Their cheeky, round faces, smiling, furry faces with big, mischievous eyes that beamed out upon the world amused and happy.

Tawney felt that here was a jolly crowd who loved a joke and would chuckle at every opportunity for a gambol.

"First," said Claudius, "we will pass among the people, so that they may all have a good look at you, then we will enter the Nest." He turned to the Courtier Bees waiting round him. "Form the procession," he said.

Immediately, a party of Guards, armed with blades of grass which they carried sloped over their shoulders like spears, took their position in front; the Colonel leading a company armed with rose-thorn swords came next; then Claudius and Tawney, walking side by side; behind them the Professor and Oswego; a party of Courtier Bees; and, finally, another troop of Guards.

"Ready?" cried Claudius.

"March!" roared the Colonel.

The procession moved forward among the buzzing crowds.

"He's a good 'un!" some one yelled.

"All pink and no fur," commented another.

"He has fur," protested a large Bee, "quite a lot of fur, on his top."

"He ought to have a tail," an elderly Bee urged. "Why, a tail would set him off proper. A big, bushy tail that 'ud make him look summut."

"Hooray!" buzzed the Bees. "Good old Claudius!"

Claudius bent his head towards Mr Tawney.

"You had better wave a paw to them," he advised. "They are overjoyed at your coming to visit them. Highly excited. That is why they forget themselves and make those impertinent remarks about my age. I make allowances, but it is highly impertinent. *I am not old.*"

"You don't look old," said Mr Tawney politely; "at least, not very."

Claudius strode along with increased dignity.

"I am in my prime," he said coldly. "Just at my best; and it is gross impertinence for them to suggest otherwise."

"Welcome!" shouted the crowd. "Hurrah! Good old Claudius!"

V

Within the Nest

Somehow Tawney had expected the Nest to be something like a cave, a rough passage under the earth, possibly dark, certainly damp. Vaguely he had thought of it as 'a hole in the ground.'

But as he walked beside Claudius in the procession he became more and more astonished. Here was no crude cavern, in fact it seemed hard to believe

one really was underground at all, for the whole place was brilliantly lit. Long rows of tubes lined the ceilings, tubes that gave off a clear blue glow not unlike daylight.

"Yes," said Claudius, in answer to Tawney's comment. "Yes, we aim to keep the whole Nest as clear as a sunny day outside. We believe that plenty of light helps to make happy Bees; gloom of any kind we do not care for. And then our lighting system is extremely simple. Those 'tubes,' as you call them, are just glow-worms. We have large farms attached to the Nest, and of course the glow-worms are glad to give their services. They have every comfort; plenty of good food, warmth, protection, and excellent quarters. A far better life for them than they would have outside. They are trained to take their proper position and to glow for an hour at a time—an hour on and three hours off. You will see them marching out of the farms, coming on duty, and the ones they have relieved marching home again. We have no trouble with them, and they are perfectly reliable."

Tawney listened eagerly.

"I thought it would be rather cold and damp," he said, "but you seem to have got it just right."

Claudius waved his paw.

"We do have some trouble," he admitted; "in very warm weather it is inclined to get, perhaps, rather too hot. Of course, we keep a steady flow of air going through; in fact, the air here is always clear and just like that outside on a summer day. We find plenty of good air keeps Bees healthy."

"But when it's damp outside, doesn't the fog come in?"

"In winter," explained Claudius, "from time to time we release supplies of midsummer air gathered during the flower season. Air collected from around roses, or honeysuckle. We store clean summer air as you store water in reservoirs."

He glanced round to see the procession was keeping in order, and then continued:

"I sometimes wonder why Humans do not live as we do. It is a very comfortable life, only when it is pleasant outside do we leave the Nest; all our friends are here in a spacious city, a city full of light and warm summer air."

They were well inside the Nest by now, marching down the main corridors, and the place reminded Tawney of a great wide street. On each side, smooth walls towered up until they met the ceiling—a ceiling so lined with light-tubes that it looked like the sky. No ugly advertisements disfigured the walls; but grouped about at intervals there were large doors and windows—doors and windows so arranged that the lines of them made a pleasant pattern and the whole effect seemed beautiful.

"The Bees live in those houses," Claudius explained. "Of course, the Nest's Architect Bees design all the houses, and so we are able to keep the whole city attractive and the design pleasing. We feel that Bees living in beautiful surroundings are gentle Bees. Now, I have often wondered why you Humans allow people to put up ugly houses. It must be very bad for people to live among horrible things."

As he spoke they came to the entrance of the Great Hall, a wide portal through which the procession passed. Claudius led the way across to the far end of the hall and then, turning round, faced the crowd that had followed and now thronged the place. The Guards and Courtier Bees formed up in a party behind Claudius.

"I see our Tailor Bees have your clothes ready," said Claudius. "Before proceeding with the ceremony it would perhaps be as well if you put them on."

Two brown Bees, carrying between them various articles of clothing, hurried forward.

"I didn't know Bees could make cloth," commented Tawney.

Claudius shook his head.

"I must admit," he said, "that fabric such as this we import from the outside world. We get it from the very best source; in fact, most of this comes from your lady mother. She has a habit of sewing things in the garden, cutting and snipping sheets of fabric, and such small pieces as she drops are usually picked up by our people and brought into the Nest."

One of the brown Bees held up a coat for Tawney's inspection. Tawney recognized the cloth as a bit from a curtain his mother had once made.

"This," began the brown Bee, "is the very latest fashion. We watch the Humans most closely, and this is exactly as now worn by Mr Allwood, who tends the flowers. The trousers we have modelled after those worn by Mr Bill, who assists him. In addition, we have a round black hat such as your good father wears—a bowl, I believe he calls it. Also a stick, black at one end."

"You mean an umbrella," suggested Tawney, eyeing the piece of straw the Bee was holding.

"I expect so," assented the Bee. "He always carries one

when leaving for the City. And, finally, we have the two strips of brown leather he carries in his paw."

"Gloves," said Tawney.

"You will be absolutely correct," murmured the Bee, as he helped Tawney to dress. "A perfect fit. A little tight round the waist, perhaps, but after wear——"

"You haven't managed to find any shoes, have you?" said Tawney, looking down at his bare feet.

The Bee waved the suggestion aside.

"Shoes," he said severely, "are not now worn. I was round the water you call the swimming-bath only on Sunday last and, believe me, sir, not one single Human was wearing shoes. Believe me, the well-dressed Human does not wear shoes to-day."

"It doesn't matter," said Tawney. "I can manage."

Claudius, who had been standing aside while the tailors had been dressing Tawney, now stepped nearer.

"A credit to the Nest," he said approvingly, as he surveyed Tawney's costume. "We will now proceed with the ceremony.

"Certain prominent citizens will now be presented to you," he told Tawney, "after which our band will play while there is a grand march round of all Bees."

"Then we have the banquet," murmured Oswego. "A special banquet."

Claudius bent over and whispered in Tawney's ear:

"Our friend Oswego thinks far too much of his stomach."

"He does look rather fat," admitted Tawney.

A tall Herald Bee now stepped forward and banged loudly with his grass staff upon the floor. For a few minutes the buzzing of the assembled Bees continued, and then, as he banged his staff once more, they hushed.

"Free Bees!" called the Herald, when there was silence, "Workers, Guards, and Gatherers of Honey, pray silence for My Lord Claudius the Bee."

As Claudius stepped forward and bowed, there was a loud buzz of applause; then as this died away, Claudius spoke.

"Bumble people, members of the Bombus family," he began, "we have with us to-day a Human, but, I venture to say, no ordinary Human . . ." There was a further buzz from the crowd, which drowned the speech for some time. " . . . I will therefore ask certain Bees to step forward and be introduced to our guest, after which there will be a grand march round, and Mr Tawney will be declared an Honorary Bee."

The Herald Bee knocked with his staff upon the floor once more, and Tawney found that Claudius and his party had withdrawn an inch or so, leaving him standing alone facing the crowd.

"Colonel Mainsting, Heather Decoration, Eater of Wasps, Destroyer of Fungus!" shouted the Herald.

And Colonel Mainsting bustled forward.

"Glad to see you, sir," he boomed. "Glad to see you safe after the outrageous incompetency"—he flung an angry glance at the unhappy Professor—"of our so-called scientists. Nincompoops, sir, that's what many of them are—nincompoops! I'm an old soldier accustomed to speak plainly—nincompoops!"

He held out his paw, and Tawney, realizing he was expected to shake hands in this way, did so.

"I'm very pleased to meet you, Colonel," he said nervously.

The Herald lifted his voice again.

"The most honourable Lord Oswego, Keeper of the Private Nectar, Devourer of Daisy Petals."

Oswego bowed low before Tawney.

"I hope you'll enjoy the banquet," he said. "There'll be special delicacies, the best that the Nest can provide. Buttercup petals dressed with clover and sprinkled with rose dew and heather honey."

"Professor Goatsbeard-Bugloss!" shouted the Herald, "Teacher of Learning, Master of Flowering Times."

The Colonel snorted audibly.

"I wonder that he has the insolence to come here

at all. A disgrace to the Nest. Letting an honoured guest . . ."

For some minutes the introductions continued. Bee after Bee came forward, offered his paw to Tawney, and then stepped back to join the little crowd around Claudius. Name after name was called, until Tawney was quite bewildered, and felt sure he would never remember them again: Captain Snapdragon, the Hon. Mrs Pond-Sedge, Sir James Dropwort-Saxifrage, Miss Juniper Loosestrife, Professor Sage Ulex.

Then the Herald seemed to pause, as if uncertain if he should call the next or not; there was a slight hush among the crowd, and the Herald lifted his voice once more.

"Black Michael of Wormwood!" he called, "Master of the Wood and Garlic."

A Bee stepped slowly forward, and it occurred to Tawney how different he seemed from the others who had greeted him.

The others had all been jolly, chuckling creatures. Some had been perhaps a little embarrassed at finding themselves so prominently in the public eye and had bumbled nervously, but about them all had been an air of happy welcome and good will. This Black Michael was different. True, as he came towards Tawney there was a smile upon his face, but it was a cunning smile, a grin that somehow reminded Tawney of some cruel spider. The lean, dark features suggested a sneaking insincerity.

"This is indeed a great honour," Black Michael purred. "No Human has ever come into a Nest before, I believe, and certainly one has never got out again. To meet anyone so clever as you, Mr Tawney, one who knows so much more than all us poor Bees, overwhelms me."

The words made Tawney feel uncomfortable; for one thing, it was difficult to find a suitable reply,

and for another, there seemed to be some veiled threat in them. Black Michael noticed Tawney hesitate, and he smirked unkindly.

"I must not take up any more of your very valuable time," he continued. "But we shall meet again, I expect. Yes, I feel sure we shall meet again."

As the dark Bee turned and stepped back again into the crowd, Claudius bent over and whispered to Oswego:

"That Bee will do with watching. I feel he means some harm to Tawney."

Oswego drew his whiskers up in surprise.

"But how could he?" he protested. "Tawney is our guest. The slightest discourtesy would be unpardonable. Why, the Bees would never forgive him."

"All the same," murmured Claudius, "I will keep my eyes on him. He has a number of followers among the idle folk."

The Herald once more raised his staff and cried:

"Free Bees, Workers, Guards, and Gatherers of Honey, the band will now play during the great march past."

Against the wall, upon a small platform raised from the floor, stood a troop of Bees. Some of these Bees carried tubes of straw in their paws and some had tiny, trumpet-shaped flowers. At the Herald's words they put these to their lips, like a man about to play a flute, and the next minute the hall rang with the boom of triumphal music. In the centre of the troop there was what Tawney decided must be a Drummer Bee, for in front of him stood two thimbles, the open ends of which were covered with tissue paper, and upon these paper ends he banged, beating time to the music of the march.

At the first note of the music the Bees had commenced to march, seven or eight in a line, orderly lines one behind the other; lifting their paws well up, nodding their heads to the music.

Tawney realized that he had heard the tune before. It was a thing called *Blaze Away*, and he had it on the gramophone at home.

Round and round the hall the Bees marched. On and on, hundreds of them, all lifting their paws in salute as they passed him, all humming and buzzing with excitement. Only when the band faded away from sheer exhaustion did they come to a stop.

"My Lord Tawney," cried Claudius, stepping forward, "Free Bees, now to the banquet!"

He rested his paw on Tawney's arm, and as the Courtier Bees and Guards of Honour formed round them, the crowds parted so that they might pass.

"Good old Claudius!" some one shouted.

There was a sudden buzz, then the whole multitude burst out into the Song of Claudius. Claudius, bowing left and right, led his party towards the banqueting-hall.

"O Claudius the Bee!
O Claudius the Bee!
Oh, what a pretty sight it is . . ."

Near the door was gathered a little party of young Bees, irresponsible young Bees with cheeky, mischievous faces. They sang with gusto:

"*Old* Claudius the Bee,
Old Claudius the Bee . . ."

Claudius pulled himself up in front of them.

"What did you say?" he demanded. "What was that you said?"

The young Bees put on a surprised expression.

"Why, we just sang 'O Claudius the Bee'!" they said innocently. "Why, what did you *think* we said?"

Claudius frowned at them.

"Never mind what I thought," he retorted.

"Just let me catch you at it again, that's all. Impudent young Bees!"

As he turned away the crowd commenced to sing again:

"O Claudius the Bee!"

But as he turned the corner the young Bees, bursting with laughter, raised their voices:

"*Old* Claudius the Bee!
Old . . ."

VI

Black Michael

As Claudius and his party reached the door of the banqueting-hall, Oswego, who had gone on ahead of them, came pushing his way back through the crowds. It was obvious that something had upset him rather seriously, for, shouldering his way through to Claudius, he drew him aside and began to whisper excitedly.

"Impossible!" cried Claudius, after a moment. "It can't be true!"

"But it is," Oswego panted. "The waiters are preparing a fresh meal, but they can't have it ready for half an hour. You'll have to put the banquet off."

"This is terrible!" said Claudius. "Our guest and all the people kept waiting. Such a thing is unheard of."

Oswego shook his head sadly.

"The waiters say," he whispered, "that they had everything ready, everything was spread out for the feast, when suddenly a few of those rough black Bees dashed into the hall. They were in and out before anyone realized what they were up to, and in the confusion they had done the damage before anyone could stop them. Just in and out. Simply swept the whole of the dishes on to the floor; wrecked the tables. Everything spoiled. There was some particularly delicious heather-dew honey. I tasted it myself."

Claudius considered the matter for a moment, then turned to Tawney.

"I cannot apologize enough," he began; "in some extraordinary way our banquet has been damaged by a few rowdy Bees. That such a thing should happen astounds me, I cannot understand it. Of course, another feast is being prepared, but I am afraid we shall have to ask you to wait for a little while. To treat a guest in this way makes me blush."

"They must have been mad," Oswego put in. "Every Bee in the Nest was invited, they have simply spoiled their own feast. And better dandelion petals I never tasted."

"I fear it is some of Black Michael's spiteful work," said Claudius, in a low voice. "I trust he means no worse trouble than this silly prank."

"Please don't worry about me," said Tawney politely, "I'm not hungry, and not in a hurry at all."

"I think," Claudius suggested, "it would be best if I showed you round the Nest while we are waiting. It would help to pass the time, and no doubt you would be interested."

Tawney smiled helpfully.

"I'm sure I should be frightfully interested," he agreed. "I should love to see the Nest."

Claudius turned to Oswego and said:

"You explain to the people. Arrange for the banquet to be held in half an hour, and in the meantime I will take our friend on a tour of the Nest."

He put his paw on Tawney's arm and drew him away. Together they moved off down the broad corridor, back towards the Great Hall.

This was a wonderful afternoon, thought Tawney some time later, really one of the most interesting times he had ever spent. It was amazing how these Bees lived. The brightly lighted rooms, the clean warm air. Every Bee they met was smiling and jolly.

Claudius took him everywhere and explained everything. They visited the glow-worm farms and saw the herds trooping in and out like cows. They visited the huge honey stores where, in thousands of wax combs, like barrels stacked one upon another, the honey was kept cool and fresh.

"There is enough food here," said Claudius, "to feed the whole Nest for at least four seasons. If anything happens, such as a wet flowering-time, which means a poor harvest, we can draw upon these stocks. All Bees are always assured of plenty."

"Don't you get frightfully tired of always eating honey?" Tawney asked.

Claudius smiled.

"If you have ever watched our people visiting your flowers you may have noticed that the same Bee never

calls upon a different kind of blossom. He never goes from, say, a Delphinium to a Dahlia, and then on to a Cornflower. Now, each variety of plant has its own particular kind of nectar, and by keeping them separate when gathering we are able to store up hundreds of different flavours. I trust I make myself clear?"

Tawney nodded.

"To a Human all honey may taste the same," Claudius continued, "but to a Bee Wallflower nectar is as different from Heather nectar as your beef is from mutton."

"I thought it was all just honey," said Tawney.

"Our people do not gather honey, they gather nectar and pollen, and it is from these—the raw materials—that we make our finished product. We manufacture honey as you make bread or cake from flour."

"You seem to know an awful lot about us," Tawney commented.

"We Bees are very observant, I may almost say curious. We spend a considerable time watching Humans in their homes. An educated Bee prides himself on understanding Human ways."

They visited the library, where the books reminded Tawney of postage-stamps, and where dozens of Bees sat chuckling over the tiny pages.

"Any Bee who wants to write books or music is given every opportunity to do so," explained Claudius. "If he has any ability the Nest encourages him. It is the same with our scientific students or our architects. Every Bee works, but every one works at the job he wants to do, and is therefore best fitted for. There is work for every one, and, because it is the job they like, all enjoy doing their share. No one is working for his own personal gain: all are working for the good of the Nest, the good of all."

For more than twenty minutes Claudius and Tawney wandered about, seeing the wonders of the place; then they came to a narrow passage cut in the solid wall, a passage just wide enough to allow one Bee to walk down it.

"I must take you down here," Claudius said. "I will go first, you follow me. This," he explained over his shoulder, "is our secret passage. It is our back way out. All Bees know of it, and in case of danger at the entrance of the Nest they can escape this way. Where this passage comes out into the garden is, of course, carefully hidden, only our own Bees can find the place. But even if anyone did discover the secret it would be a very easy place to defend. One Bee could hold a narrow passage like this against an army."

They pushed on down the dimly lighted corridor until a faint glimmer of daylight appeared ahead.

"Careful here," Claudius warned; "we go through a low doorway, and beyond is quite a large room. There will be a sentry on guard in the room."

He stooped down to pass through the low doorway and disappeared inside. Tawney followed close behind him.

"I can't understand where the sentry is," murmured Claudius. "He should have——"

There was a loud bang behind them as a door slammed and a bolt shot into place.

"Got you!" said a voice. "Got you both! You're trapped!"

2

There was hardly a struggle. The attack was so sudden, so unexpected, that almost before either Claudius or Tawney realized there was anything wrong they were flung down upon the floor and were bound with strong cords. Tawney tried to force the bindings, driving his arms and legs against the cords, but it seemed useless; a dozen beasts, whose strength seemed enormous, were busy tying him firmly. They worked in silence, and except for the panting of their breath there was not a sound.

Claudius was the first to speak.

"You, Black Michael!" he said. "I might have guessed."

Black Michael, who had been dancing about on the outskirts of the skirmish, gave a sneering laugh.

"Yes, me, Black Michael. I planned it all, and now I've got you. I've been polite to your face for months, and all the time I've hated——"

"But Bees can't hate," interrupted Claudius. "No sane Bee ever hates."

Black Michael kicked savagely at the tied-up body lying helpless on the floor.

"You mean I'm mad!" he stormed. "Me mad, Black Michael, the greatest being on earth, the strongest, the cleverest . . ."

He kicked out once again, and putting a foot on Claudius's stomach, drove it down with his full weight.

"I've watched you prancing about and I've hated you all, all the grinning Bees with their silly jokes.

Now I've got you, and soon I'm going to take my rightful place. Black Michael, Master of the Nest!"

"I should have guessed," gasped Claudius; "I ought to have known something was wrong when the sentry did not challenge us."

"The sentry!" Black Michael laughed hysterically.

Tawney caught a glimpse of a crumpled body lying in a heap by the door.

"Oh, he's dead!" he cried.

"Yes, dead!" shouted Black Michael.

"This is murder," said Claudius seriously. "To kill a fellow Bee——"

"Dead, dead, dead!" howled Black Michael. "And you'll be dead soon, and this filthy Human you've dragged into the Nest as well."

Claudius struggled into a sitting position and surveyed the dozen or so of dark Bees that clustered round him.

"Listen to me," he said. "All this is madness. Soon we shall be missed from the Nest. You must realize what the people will be like when they know you have ill-treated their guest. They will force the passage and——"

"Listen to me," said Black Michael, speaking for the first time in a soft, cooing voice. "Not all the army, with that foul Mainsting at its head, can force the passage. You know that three or four of us can hold it easily; that's the way the passage was built, to keep out intruders. Ah, you think, well, when they find us holding the passage, they'll go round to the secret entrance in the garden and attack from there. Well, if they do, they'll find my friends the wasps there. A nice surprise for Mainsting to find a hundred wasps waiting for him."

Claudius lifted his voice in horror.

"You haven't—you couldn't——" he stammered. "You haven't shown the wasps the secret entrance to the Nest?"

Black Michael's wild laugh answered him.

"Now I know you're mad," said Claudius slowly. "That is treason to the Nest. Treason and murder."

"And I'll tell you something else," said Black Michael; "I'll tell you what we're going to do. As soon as we had you safely captured, one of my men flew off to tell the wasps our plan had been successful, and to bring them here. When they come, they will hide quietly in this passage until another army of wasps attacks the main entrance. Then they will steal down the passage and make a surprise attack. The Nest will be attacked back and front, and Mainsting won't have a chance. A lot of the Bees will be killed and the rest forced to submit. Then the wasps will take their payment in honey, and will declare me, Black Michael, Master, and I shall rule in your place."

"You fool!" cried Claudius passionately. "Do you think the wasps will leave the Nest until they have taken everything? Once inside they will destroy the whole place. Who can stop them? Not you and your paltry men. Why, they'll probably kill you off first."

Black Michael stamped angrily.

"I will not have such talk!" he shouted. "No one can kill me. I am Black Michael. But I'll tell you what is going to happen to you. When the wasps come, they are going to get hold of your wings and your paws and pull them off. One by one, pull them off your body, until only a head and a trunk are left. The great Claudius, without legs or wings, not able to fly or walk!"

Claudius was silent for a moment.

"Whatever you do to me seems beyond help," he said. "It is the fate of the Nest that terrifies me, the Nest and this guest of ours. Do what you will, but him, at least, you must see to safety. He has done harm to none. He is not concerned with the Bumble folk's troubles. Well you know how wasps hate Humans; if once they come and find him here . . . I implore you, take him quickly to the secret entrance and speed him away."

"He can die slowly and horribly," said Black Michael carelessly, "die any way the wasps wish, as far as I am concerned."

There was silence for a few moments in the darkness. The black Bees were watching Claudius, hardly heeding the trussed-up Human who lay upon the floor.

Tawney prised at the cords that bound him; with all his strength he heaved and pressed against the bonds. Suddenly, one cord seemed to give a little. Tawney wriggled cautiously, drew his fingers tightly together, and found he could slip the fastenings from his wrists. Carefully now, one quick jerk before the dark Bees could stop him, and he might be able to tear off the cords from his legs. He drew himself together for one great effort.

There came a noise from the end of the room where the daylight showed.

"Black Michael!" a voice called.

The wasps had come.

VII

The Wasps

THEY were horrible creatures, those wasps. The vivid-coloured stripes on their bodies seemed to be put there by Nature as a warning of the cruel beast they marked. They were not furry like the Bees, but had a smooth covering that glistened like armour and clicked at the joints as they walked. Lean and thin, they looked both powerful and savage.

"So you managed to bring your plan off all right?" commented the leading wasp, striding towards Black Michael. "And this is the secret passage, is it? Well, it won't be secret long now. I've got fifty wasps following me here, and in fifteen minutes the attack on the front entrance will begin. Then

we'll come down the passage and surprise every one."

He laughed, and it seemed to Tawney he had never heard a more dreadful sound.

"And as soon as you've captured the Nest you'll make the Bees declare me Master?" demanded Black Michael.

The wasp did not reply.

"You promised," Black Michael said anxiously. "It was arranged."

"There may be no Bees left when we've finished," muttered the wasp. Then he bent down and stared at Claudius. "So this is the great Claudius, is it? Well, he doesn't look much now, and in half an hour or so he'll look even worse."

"I mean to have his wings and legs pulled off!" shrieked Black Michael. "Let your wasps start doing it now."

The chief wasp bent lower; then, with a laugh, he spat deliberately into Claudius's face.

"My wasps aren't going to wear themselves out pulling a flea like this about," he said. "At least, not now. After we've captured the Nest and got the honey we'll see to him—and some others too. But for the next ten minutes my wasps are going to rest, sleep if they can, so as to be fresh when the fighting starts."

Black Michael commenced to argue; the wasp cut him short.

"You shut up!" he said roughly. "I'm in charge here. There's going to be hard fighting, and I mean to have rested men to do it." He turned and drove his shoulder against Black Michael, so that Black Michael stumbled and almost fell. "Where's this filthy Human?" he continued. "Let's have a look at the beast."

He strode over to Tawney and glared down at him.

"Yes, you'll do like that until I'm ready to settle with you," he sneered. "You're tied up all right."

Tawney saw the ugly fangs that protruded from the wasp's mouth, and shuddered; there was a rank smell from his breath that made Tawney feel sick.

"I've half a mind to plunge my sting into the Human beast now," the wasp rasped. "Sting him until he's dead, the flea. How I hate Humans! Still, stinging's too quick for him. When we've finished the Nest off, we'll try something really slow. Something as painful as we can make it. Pull his teeth and nails out first."

He turned away regretfully.

"Now, all you lot, ten minutes' rest before the attack. D'you hear me!"

Black Michael ventured to protest.

"Oughtn't we to leave a sentry on guard?" he said.

The wasp swung round upon him suddenly:

"Wither my wings! Do you think you know better than I, you fool? When I rasp, let no dog bark. One more croak, and I run my sting into you."

Black Michael cowered against the wall.

"Now then, sleep!" ordered the wasp. "A rested wasp is worth four tired ones, and my men have been working all day. They're not far off worn-out."

Tawney watched the wasps settle down against the wall; watched them slump their great heads between their shoulders. One or two of them scratched with a leg at some flea upon their backs; one coughed noisily, then spat out upon the floor. Gradually, the room became silent. The Bees cowered down, looking only at the resting wasps.

It was almost dark in the room; only the faint glimmer of daylight from the end of the passage lightened the gloom.

If he could get his hands free and manage to untie his feet, thought Tawney, there was a chance—a slight chance—that he might be able to crawl to the opening unobserved. Gently he worked at the cords binding his wrists, then, as he contrived to draw his hands free, bent slowly forward until his fingers touched the knots holding his ankles.

A minute later he was crawling silently towards the daylight.

2

That crawl across the darkness of the room is something that Tawney will never forget. Wriggling along in the shadow of the wall, terrified that some sound or movement would attract attention, expecting every second to be seen and pounced upon. . . .

It seemed ages before he reached the passage and, climbing to his feet, ran cautiously towards the daylight.

The secret entrance was in some tall grass, cleverly hidden so that even some one who knew its position might have difficulty in finding it, while a passer-by would never have suspected its existence. Tawney, when he came through the low doorway, sprang quickly towards the grass and pushed his way into its shelter. Like trees, the grass towered above and hid him as if he were deep in a forest. Tawney hurried on, stumbling over the roots; sometimes a great boulder blocked his path, and as he dodged around one of these Tawney realized it was just a stone like one of those pebbles which, in his ordinary life, he often kicked aside with his foot.

He came at last to the edge of the tall grass—it was really little more than a patch about the size of a table-cloth—struggled across a bed of soft raked earth, and reached the smooth lawn beyond. It was easy to walk here, the grass—it had been mown only yesterday—hardly reached to his knees, and as he hurried towards the house he could see Allwood, the gardener, clipping a hedge. Tawney listened to the clip-clip of the shears and felt he was safe. If the wasps came after him now, a shout would attract Allwood's attention; yes, he was safe. . . .

Then, suddenly, something seemed to change in Tawney's mind. He had escaped, but what about Claudius? What about the Nest? He imagined the wasps destroying everything, pouring out the honey, killing, tearing up. The idea of Claudius dying in that dark room made Tawney feel as if he were going to cry. They would kill him slowly, cruelly. At the thought of this, the fear Tawney had felt for the wasps seemed to leave him, and in its place came a hatred for the beasts that were about to attack his small friends.

"They shan't do it!" he cried aloud. "I'll stop them in some way. Yes, I will."

His mind worked rapidly. Anything Allwood could do would be useless. Suppose he attracted Allwood's attention—the gardener would be so astonished to see Tawney at his present size that a long time must be lost explaining and urging. No. Allwood would never understand. Then again, at the first sign of a clumsy attack by a Human, the wasps would murder Claudius in the passage.

It came clearly to Tawney that he was the only one who could save Claudius. He must go back to the secret entrance, creep in, and take the wasps unawares. He must fight them and win. There was no terror in his heart now, only a fear that he might be too late, and a great loathing for the wasps.

As he made up his mind, he suddenly remembered something that had happened earlier in the day. His mother had been carrying her sewing-basket down the garden, and the lid had come undone. All the contents had fallen out on to the lawn. Tawney remembered just where this had happened, he had helped to pick them up—among the things that had fallen out had been a lot of needles. Needles—sharp steel needles: for a man only an inch high, a perfect sword.

Tawney raced over to where the sewing-basket had been upset. It was as he had expected. All the things had not been picked up, two bright needles glittered on the grass. Taking the longer one as a sword, and the shorter as a dagger, Tawney turned back towards the forest of tall grass.

Two minutes later he was creeping in through the secret entrance.

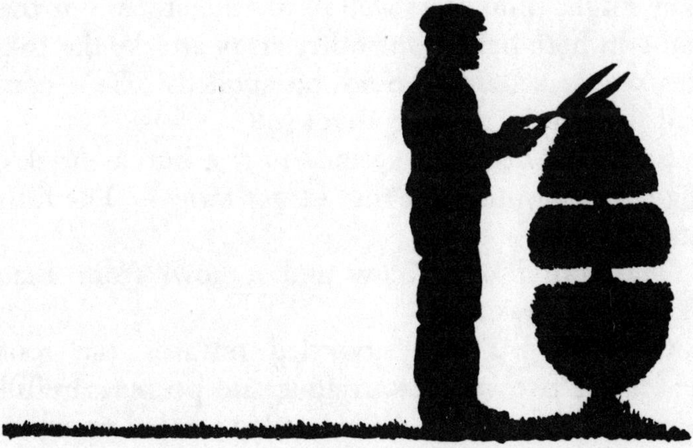

VIII

The Fight

As he slipped into the passage Tawney heard the wasps murmuring in the room beyond. The voice of the head wasp rose above the disturbance.

"I tell you," it rasped, "he's got away. I've been right down the passage, right to the entrance, and there isn't a sign of the filthy flea."

It seemed to Tawney that Black Michael made some suggestion, but the wasp interrupted him.

"No, we'll not go out and look for him," said the wasp; "because we might be noticed. If Mainsting's Guards saw a wasp near the secret entrance they might think it as well to investigate, and if they came in here before our other army attacks the front the whole scheme would be spoiled. He's gone, and we can do nothing about it."

Suddenly his voice seemed to rise into a shriek of rage: "It's your fault that he got away! The filthy little flea!"

The sound of a blow and a howl from Black Michael followed.

Cautiously Tawney crawled towards the room where the two were quarrelling and peered carefully round the doorway. Claudius lay trussed up in one corner, Black Michael and his few dark Bees cowered miserably against a wall; the wasps stood about the floor, scratching themselves and spitting, as if impatient for the fighting to begin.

"I'll get him again!" stormed the head wasp. "I'll get him. I'll see the little flea some time, and then I'll tear him into pieces. No one hates Humans more than I do. I've stung more Humans——" He stopped speaking and strolled towards Claudius. "Anyway, there's still this old Bee left to deal with," he added.

Claudius raised his head.

"Sir," he said firmly, "I'll trouble you to understand that I am *not* old."

As if enraged by the remark, the wasp seized one of the tied Bee's legs.

"You won't escape, anyway!" he shouted. "I'll pull your wings off now." He turned to his men: "Come on, give me a pull with this beast."

Tawney slipped quickly across the room. So occupied were the wasps with their horrible intention that Tawney was right behind the leader before anyone realized he was there.

"Now, a long, slow pull, I'll——"

"No, you won't!" said Tawney.

The wasps leapt round in surprise. For a second or so there was silence, then the head wasp growled out a curse.

"So you didn't escape?" he muttered. "Well,

I'll finish you off this time. I'll break your legs first——"

The point of Tawney's sword drove him suddenly backward.

"I give you one chance," said Tawney. "Get out! Go now, by the secret entrance, the whole lot of you, and I'll not harm anyone."

He stepped over to Claudius and stood above him, on guard.

"Outside!" ordered Tawney.

The head wasp, who had backed with his followers out of range of the sword-point, shook his head.

"There's no need to be angry about things," he said. "After all, it was only a joke; you don't suppose we should have touched dear Claudius or really damaged the Nest?"

"You get out!" said Tawney. "And take your creatures with you."

The head wasp put on a hurt expression.

"The whole thing's a misunderstanding. We never intended to really hurt anyone. That is not a wasp's way. No, sir."

Tawney cut him short.

"You go and tell your friends," he commanded, "that it will be a waste of time to attack the front of the Nest. I shall guard this passage while Claudius goes and warns Colonel Mainsting."

"Well, well," said the wasp, grinning through his fangs, "you've beaten us, and I suppose it can't be helped. Yes, there seems nothing more we can do. I harbour no ill-will; in fact, I admire your courage. Let us part like gentlewasps; let us shake paws."

For a moment Tawney hesitated. The wasp saw this, and commenced pleading again.

"I'm sorry for what's happened, and I give you my word I'm your friend now. I know a brave man when I see one. You can trust me. Why, I wouldn't harm you for anything."

He moved forward towards where Tawney stood.

"All fighting's finished," he urged. "We're beaten and bear no malice. All I ask is that we part friends. Let us shake paws."

The wasp came closer, and after a moment of indecision Tawney lowered his sword and stretched out his hand.

There was a sudden cry from Claudius.

"Look out!" he shouted.

Startled by the cry, Tawney jumped aside and ducked; the wasp's sting whistled over his head. With fangs and sting bared, the wasp sprang again.

There was a flash of steel, a click as the needle pierced the hard shell of the beast, and then, as Tawney drew his sword out again, the wasp collapsed in a heap upon the floor.

"You've killed him!" shouted Black Michael.

Tawney stood on guard, expecting the other wasps to attack. There were many of them, and he felt that if they all came on at once he would have little chance, but there was no retreat now. The fight was on, a fight to the finish. The wasps, however, did not advance, they hung back, muttering and spitting.

"Outside!" said Tawney, after a moment.

They stood before him, hesitating. Tawney took a step forward, the point of his sword in a line with the foremost wasp's head. With a howl, Black Michael turned and fled towards the entrance.

"I've had enough," he stammered.

The dark Bees ran quickly after him, then the wasps, with a final grumble, followed. A moment later they were pushing their way towards the entrance.

2

As the last wasp disappeared, Tawney bent down and commenced tugging at the cords which bound Claudius.

"You have saved the Nest and you have saved my life," said Claudius.

"Are you all right?" asked Tawney anxiously. "They didn't hurt you, did they?"

Claudius waved the inquiry aside.

"You were safe outside. You came back into the greatest danger and saved the Nest. Nothing the Bumble folk can do will ever repay you. They will be crazy with gratitude."

"I was awfully frightened," admitted Tawney.

"Only the fool does not know fear," Claudius replied. "The brave Bee is the one who is frightened but who does not show it."

"We ought to hurry," said Tawney, struggling to undo the cords; "we must warn Colonel Mainsting."

Claudius shook his head.

"There is no need to hurry now. Once the wasps know they have failed at this secret passage they will not attack the Nest. Mainsting and his Guards would eat them if they attacked the front. It was only this plan to capture the passage and surprise our people from the back that gave them any chance. Now our workers will close this passage up and dig another one somewhere else. The Nest is saved."

As Tawney undid the last knot, Claudius shook himself free of the cords and, climbing to his feet, stretched his wings.

"It was most fortunate for you, Mr Tawney, that

our people were not destroyed. Without our scientists you would never have got back to your large size again."

Tawney had not thought of that. To have been forced to go home no bigger than a keyhole. . . .

"I must say," Claudius continued, "that the enormous size Humans adopt must be very awkward and uncomfortable. But still, I suppose you get used to it in time; I expect you hardly notice how unpleasant it is. One gets used to anything."

While they were speaking there came a faint rustle from the dark corner beside the far wall. Both Tawney and Claudius heard it and instantly sprang round. Tawney raised his sword in front of him.

"What's that?" cried Claudius anxiously.

Something moved in the gloom. A figure began to crawl towards them.

"It's the sentry!" shouted Tawney. "They didn't kill him."

The Sentry Bee pushed himself along the floor towards them and then climbed to his feet. He stood before them, rubbing his furry head with his paws.

"They socked me," he complained; "crept up behind me, they did, and socked me over the head. You wait until I catch that Black Michael; you wait, that's all."

"We thought you were dead," said Claudius. "Did they hurt you?"

The sentry rolled his eyes.

"O' course they hurt me. I tell you they socked me over the head. But you just wait until I meet that grinning Michael. I'll clock him one that 'ull knock him into next summer."

"I cannot bring myself to blame you," Claudius remarked. "He is a bad Bee and deserves a sharp lesson. I also have had my troubles; he and his ruffians laid violent paws upon me."

"I hope you really feel all right?" Tawney said politely. "At your age a shock like this——"

Claudius drew himself up.

"I do not understand you. I am still a long way from middle age."

"I didn't mean——" Tawney began.

"I'm sure you didn't," said Claudius; "and even

if you did, I remember what the Nest owes to you. I could forgive you anything—even telling me I am past my best." He chuckled good-humouredly. "Now, let us go back; our people will be beginning to look for us."

As he spoke, there came the sound of some Bees running down the passage. A moment later Colonel Mainsting, at the head of a party of Guards, rushed into the room.

"You're safe!" he cried.

Then he caught sight of the dead wasp.

"Balsam and dandelions! Vespa vulgaris!" he roared. "What has happened?"

"I'll tell you everything" said Claudius soothingly, "and when I do . . ."

IX

Banquet

THE banquet was nearly over. Tawney, sitting beside Claudius at the head of the great table, looked round and felt glad the meal was coming to an end—he could not have eaten anything more. All down the tables the Bees—like rows of brown, woolly Teddy Bears—were pushing aside their plates and sitting back replete after this sumptuous feast. Even Oswego had almost finished and now only toyed lightly with a dish of daisy pollen.

It had all been terribly exciting, thought Tawney. Colonel Mainsting's fury when he learned of Black Michael's treachery and the attack on Claudius and Tawney; it was with the greatest difficulty that he had been prevented from leading his Guards out to war upon the wasps. The amazement of the Bees when they learned the story of the adventure. Their excitement when they realized Tawney had saved the Nest. Almost mad they had been. Tawney looked at the rows of smiling faces, chuckling at one another's jokes, and could hardly believe that this was the wild mob that had carried him shoulder-high while they howled thanks and praises, mixed with defiant threats about Black Michael and the wasps.

"Now that our banquet is ending," said Claudius, "I think we might have a little music. We Bumble folk are all keen musicians, and we shall be able to play you music just as you hear it among the Humans. Indeed, our composers often visit your house when the Henry-Hall box is working, and many are the pretty tunes they bring back with them. Not so delightful as our own Bee music, I think myself, but still, many of our young people—I mean, many of our people enjoy them."

He waved his paws and then, as all the Bees seemed too much occupied with their fun to heed him, banged loudly upon the table.

"The band," he called. "Let the band play for our guest."

There was a shout of approval, and the members of the band, hurriedly finishing their cups of nectar, rose, and stumbled to where their instruments lay. A moment later the hall shook to the notes of Schubert's *Marche Militaire*, while the Bees stamped their paws and banged in time to the music. Claudius hummed an accompaniment to the triumphal tune of victory.

Claudius in Jovial Mood

"Perhaps you sing yourself?" he said, as the music ended. "Every Bee would be delighted if you cared to raise your voice."

The Banquet

"Oh, no," Tawney replied hurriedly. "I'm not good at all at singing—at least, not before a crowd like this. I'd much rather not, thank you all the same."

Claudius nodded his understanding.

"Just as you wish. I will ask one of our people who is an expert on Human songs to sing for us." He rose to his feet again and called "A song for our guest. I ask one of our Human music performers to give voice. Perhaps Regional Harebell will oblige."

The Bees greeted the proposal with delight, and when the buzzing subsided a large brown Bee mounted the platform where the band was seated and instructed them regarding the accompaniment they were to play.

"One of our best Human singers," commented Claudius. "He specializes in your songs. Indeed, he is always round your windows listening and learning. He will sing you a Human song exactly as it is played among your people. You won't know the difference."

The brown Bee, having spoken to the band and made sure they understood just what he proposed to sing, came slowly to the front of the platform and bowed solemnly right and left.

"*This is the National Programme*,"

he announced briskly. "*Before singing the song there are two statements and a polite message. Will Oswego, the Bee, last heard of eating a third plate of clover tips, go at once from the hall, where his noisy eating will not disturb the listeners.*"

"Wonderful," whispered Claudius. "It might be the Henry-Hall box itself."

The brown Bee, having made his announcement, signalled to the band to commence, and began his song, and at the first few words Tawney felt bewildered. He was too polite to say anything, but as he listened, and saw all the Bees swinging to the rhythm, Tawney felt sure the singer had made some mistake over the words:

> "*I'm lovely to look at,*
> *Delightful to know,*
> *And wonderfully sweet to kiss;*
> *A combination like this*
> *Is nice as ever a thing can be,*
> *Imagine finding a dream like me.*
> *I'm lovely to look at,*
> *Delightful to know,*
> *And terribly tight,*
> *For we're together, the moon we see,*
> *And oh it's lovely to look at me—To-night.*"

The Bees obviously enjoyed the performance, and when in the middle of the song the singer put in three shrill 'pips' Claudius nodded proudly.

"He is remarkably gifted," he murmured. "Even remembering those strange squeaks Humans insert in their music."

"But," whispered Tawney, "those aren't really part of the song, those 'pips' are the time-signal; they have them on the wireless to let people know ——"

"I do not understand Human music sufficiently to appreciate them myself," Claudius interrupted; "but no doubt you Humans find them an attractive addition."

Tawney decided it was best to say no more. It seemed impossible to explain.

As the singer finished, loud applause arose, and, bowing to the buzzing audience, he made another announcement:

"*You have been listening to Regional Harebell and his voice broadcasting to you from the Bumble Bees' Banqueting Hall. We have just played to you 'I'm lovely to look at.'*"

"Exactly as you have it at home," said Claudius, with satisfaction in his voice. "He might be Human; not a single mistake."

"It's very interesting," said Tawney, who did not wish to argue.

"It is not our custom for a Bee to sing twice at the same performance," explained Claudius, "but I do wish you could have heard him sing *I'm Devon, Glorious Devon*. He sings that remarkably well."

"I'm sure he does," said Tawney.

2

The banquet and concert came to an end at last, and while most of the Bees pushed their way from the hall, a few of the more important ones gathered around Tawney and Claudius.

"I must confess I am a little concerned about our friend Claudius," said Professor Goatsbeard-Bugloss. "I fear the anxious time through which he has passed has affected his health."

"I do feel a trifle tired," admitted Claudius.

"What you want," remarked Oswego, "is feeding up. Plenty of nourishing food."

The Professor shook his head.

"The strain to which he has been subjected," he said, "has been considerable. At his age——"

"I feel quite well," interrupted Claudius sharply.

"But, my dear sir," the Professor continued, "the terrible time you spent with those wasps, your anxiety for the safety of the Nest, is bound to tell upon you. It is a proven fact that an old Bee——"

Claudius cut the speaker short

"I'll trouble you," he said, "not to refer to me as 'an old Bee'! I am in my prime, and I shall be obliged if every one will remember it."

He glared round at the assembled Bees.

"I didn't mean——" began the Professor.

Colonel Mainsting brushed him aside.

"You don't know what you *do* mean," he said fiercely. "Half your time you're dreaming and fancying. First you mismanage the arrival of our guest, and now you insult Claudius here. Why, confound it, sir, in the Guards, Bees have been dismissed the service for less. Let me tell you, sir, I consider you little better than a rascally wasp. Just because an old Bee like Claudius feels——"

It seemed to Tawney it was time for him to intervene.

"When my father doesn't feel well," said Tawney, "he goes away for a sea-cruise. He says the rest does him good."

Claudius rubbed a paw across his forehead.

"A cruise would certainly be a novelty," he said. "I don't believe any Bee has yet been for a cruise."

"Such a change would be most beneficial," remarked the Professor softly.

"And," put in Oswego, "I've heard they feed you remarkably well on boats."

"You meet interesting people, too," added Tawney. "On the last cruise, my father met an American girl, and she . . ."

Claudius looked thoughtfully around him.

"I wish I could go," he said. "I wish we could all go; but it does not seem possible."

Suddenly Tawney had an idea.

"But it is," he cried. "It is possible. I'll tell you how we can all go on a cruise."

The Bees gathered closer, rubbing their paws with excitement, their woolly, smiling faces twitching with interest.

"Be so good, sir," ordered Colonel Mainsting, "as to explain your plan of campaign. I am a soldier, sir, not a sailor, but if duty calls me to travel on the sea, why, confound it, sir, then I'll travel on it."

"It'll be quite easy," said Tawney; "let me tell you how we can arrange it all."

And for five minutes he talked, explaining, while the Bees nodded approval and delight.

X

Cruising Home

THE whole Nest was buzzing with excitement. Bees hurried hither and thither, chattering and calling to one another.

"My dear," cooed a slim young Bee with bright golden fur, "how can I possibly go without having my hair done?"

"Oh, I think it's just *too* twilling," lisped another. "I shall send postcards from all the ports and . . ."

One of the Guard Bees, a sergeant, regarded the bustling crowds gloomily.

"It's 'ard," he grumbled. "'Ard, that's what it is. Me going to sea at my time o' life. Me, mind you, chief steward on a pleasure cruise!" He

paused to spit disgustedly, and then continued: "Me running round with plates o' food on a ship, mind you. Me! Why, back in the old days, when I was a young Bee in the second 'Eather Campaign . . ."

"I do hope I shall be warm enough," a big brown Bee commented. "I'm taking my thickest fur."

"I have an excellent remedy for sea-sickness," remarked Professor Goatsbeard-Bugloss, "if anyone feels the least indisposed. Perhaps you, my dear Colonel, would care to try some?"

Colonel Mainsting brushed him aside.

"Confound it, sir! Let me tell you that a Guard is never sick. I'd like to catch the Bee in my regiment who dared to be sick. I'd make an example of the cad; make an example of him, sir."

Claudius surveyed the scene and then, turning, laid his paw on Tawney's arm.

"It will be a most enjoyable adventure for us

all," he said. "Every Bee will be most grateful to you."

Tawney glanced down at his smart blue uniform, and, lifting his hand, settled the gold-braided peaked cap more firmly on his head.

"It will be great fun for me," he said. "I've always wanted to sail a big liner, but, of course, when I was my normal size it was impossible."

Claudius nodded.

"We ought to call at different ports," Tawney continued, "and the passengers ought to go sight-seeing and buy souvenirs. My father once went shopping with a lady at Casablanca, but he said that fortunately it was a Sunday, and they couldn't buy anything. Only look in the shop-windows."

"You're sure you understand how to sail this—what do you call it?"

"Scale-model," explained Tawney. "My father

made it after he came back from a cruise. It's the exact copy of the *Vandyck*. Like those models you see in glass cases on railway-stations."

"It is not my custom to frequent railway-stations," corrected Claudius.

"Anyway," said Tawney, "it's a perfect model, and will be just like a big liner to people of our size. I shall love being Captain and directing things from the bridge. I was sailing it on the pond after lunch, and I left it there, meaning to bring it in later."

"You look very smart in that uniform," Claudius commented. "I'm glad our people were able to make it for you so quickly."

Tawney felt a little embarrassed.

"I think," he said, "I'd better be getting on board. There's a lot to see to. Oswego's already gone aboard to superintend all the food arrangements. It was a splendid idea to make him purser."

2

The scale-model *Vandyck* rocked gently by the bank of the pond. On the bridge, Tawney, his

head just showing above the bulwark, watched the crew making ready to cast off and the stewards hurrying the last of the passenger Bees aboard. He could not help smiling to himself at the quaint picture the Bees made. Those who were acting as crew and stewards had fitted themselves with tiny round sailors' caps, and the solemn way they bustled about their duties, the caps perched on the top of their round, furry heads, made Tawney want to laugh aloud.

As the last of the passengers were coming aboard, Tawney walked off the bridge on to the boat deck, where four Bees stood waiting by the electric motor-switch.

"You quite understand what you've to do?" he asked.

"Aye, aye, sir," the Bees responded.

"Watch for my orders from the bridge," Tawney warned them.

"Aye, aye, sir!"

"Are the four Bees who are going to work the rudder ready?"

"Four Sea Bees are on duty at the rudder, sir," came the reply reprovingly.

Cruising Home H

Tawney glanced round. The liner rocked in the sunlight as the waves lapped her sides. The last gangway was pulled up. He walked briskly back to the bridge.

"Cast off!" he shouted. "Half-speed ahead! Hard-a-starboard with that rudder!"

There came a gentle tremor as the motor began to revolve and the hull quivered to its vibration. Slowly the ship began to move. The bow swung away from the shore, came gradually round, and as the ship turned towards the open water the land slipped astern.

"Full speed ahead!" called Tawney. "Port your helm! Keep her at that."

The *Vandyck*, with its load of Bees, passenger Bees, officer Bees, stewards, and crew, had commenced its cruise.

From below came the sound of Oswego the purser's voice:

"I am exceedingly sorry, madam; I will see what can be done to oblige you. Of course, the Captain's table is already full, but perhaps. . . . Yes, sir, I will attend to it at once; no doubt we can find you another cabin farther aft. . . . Certainly, Colonel, I will arrange for a meeting of the Sports Committee immediately. . . ."

From the bow look-out came a shrill cry: "Water-lilies on the port bow!"

"Starboard a little!" ordered Tawney.

3

That cruise was a great success.

The weather was perfect, warm, pleasant sunshine; and the Bees, strolling about the decks and crowding to the ship's side, enjoyed themselves thoroughly. Colonel Mainsting endeavoured to organize 'Passenger Sports,' but as most of the Bees were too busy watching the unusual sights to bother with 'Sports,' in the end the prizes were given to the only three Bees who had competed, two young Bees with bright golden fur and Colonel Mainsting.

Directed by Tawney the ship cruised about the pond, round the big islands of water-lilies, across to the waterfall where the stream tumbled in over great lumps of rock—dangerous rocks and swirling currents which made Tawney anxious for the safety of his ship. However, the Bees worked the rudder, and the motor-switch behaved so well, obeying so promptly the commands from the bridge, that everything went off perfectly; and when at last the *Vandyck* headed for open water again, and Tawney realized that evening was coming on, and that the cruise must end, he felt really disappointed. It was great fun, he thought, to stand up here on the bridge and cause the model to stop or turn just as one wanted.

Time went by, and in due course the ship came in sight of the bank where the passengers had embarked. All the Bees crowded to the ship's rails to see the land as Tawney prepared to manœuvre her alongside.

"Half-speed ahead!" he ordered. "Hard-a-port! Starboard a little. Keep her like that."

Suddenly there came a frantic buzz from the forward deck.

"Bee overboard!"

Tawney rushed to the side of the bridge. There

in the water, far down below the tall side of the ship, Professor Goatsbeard-Bugloss struggled. Leaning over, inquisitive as ever, the Professor had fallen overboard.

"Full speed astern!" shouted Tawney. "Throw him a lifebelt. Lower a boat."

On the deck below, the Bees, wildly excited at the accident, buzzed and tumbled over each other.

"'E'll drown," said one of the Bees, who was dressed as a chief steward. "Drown, that 'e will."

"Why doesn't some one do something?" howled Oswego.

As he spoke, there was a startled cry, a cry so loud that it seemed to silence the buzzing of all the Bees. A brown figure, like a brown ball, tumbled from the rail, and with a splash hit the water.

"Colonel Mainsting!" breathed Tawney. "Jumped in to rescue him." He turned as Claudius ran swiftly up on to the bridge. "There's no real danger," he continued. "Really, Claudius, they're quite safe. No need for the Colonel to have gone to the rescue. We'll have them both out in a moment."

By now the ship had come almost to a standstill, and already Sailor Bees were dangling cords overboard within reach of the two struggling Bees.

"Don't worry," urged Tawney, as Claudius clutched his arm. "See, Mainsting and the Professor have caught hold of the ropes. They're

pulling them on board again now. Come along with me."

Together, Tawney and Claudius hurried down to the deck where, hampered by the buzzing passengers, the sailors were hauling at the ropes they had thrown into the water. As Tawney, pushing his way through the crowd, reached the ship's rail the Professor, clinging to a rope, struggled on to the deck again. A moment later Colonel Mainsting also appeared.

"A most noble act," said Claudius, "a very noble act; Colonel Mainsting, you are a brave Bee. You saw our friend in danger; without a thought for your own safety you plunged to his assistance. The Nest is proud of you."

There was a loud roar of applause from the crowd.

"A brave Bee! Hurrah for Mainsting!"

For some seconds the Colonel stood there shaking the water from his fur, growling fiercely.

"We are proud of you," announced Claudius.

The Colonel gave a roar.

"D'you think I was fool enough to jump over of my own free will?" he burst out. "I never jumped, I was pushed. Pushed, sir. That nincompoop was never in any danger. I was watching his absurd antics in the water, and I was *pushed.*" He turned upon the unfortunate Professor, who was slinking away into the crowd. "Confound it, sir, you play one fool trick after another. You behave like a bally gnat, I say. Look at my fur, sir. Let me tell you your impudence . . ."

"Full speed ahead!" called Tawney. "Passengers get ready to go ashore."

XI

Before the Story ends

EVERY Bee who lived in the Nest had gathered outside the entrance. They stood packed shoulder to shoulder, pressed together like seeds upon a tray. But it was a silent crowd, a crowd among which no Bee spoke to his neighbour, a crowd where each stared in front of him, sad and sorry.

The time had come for Tawney to leave the Bees.

"It is getting late, and we may delay no longer," said Claudius. "What our feelings are I need not dwell upon. You came to us a stranger, you leave us a friend of every Bee in the Nest. When you have gone back to your own life we shall remember and think of the little Human we have learned to love."

Claudius paused to wipe a tear from his bushy eyelashes, and Tawney, watching him, wondered if it would be very rude to say how much he resented being called 'a little Human.'

"Wherever Bees buzz, the name of Tawney will be thought of with gratitude and affection," Claudius went on. "You saved our Nest; the Free Bee people never forget."

He stopped speaking and signed to Oswego to come forward and express his thanks.

"Some one ought to say something," began Oswego, "but I don't know what to say. It has been wonderful having Tawney with us; we've had some of the best banquets I ever remember. Those clover petals were a delight, and better nectar I have never tasted, while the flavour of the buttercup pollen——"

Colonel Mainsting, who had been listening impatiently, brushed him aside.

"I'm an old Bee," he began, "who has served his Nest in many parts of the garden, and I am accustomed to say plainly what I mean. I want to tell you, sir, we're proud to have had you with us. Your behaviour when those rascally wasps appeared was that of a Bee, a true Bee. I say it, and I'd like to see the half-wit who'd contradict me."

He glared round as if hoping that some Bee in the crowd would take up the challenge.

"There is no time for more talk," said Claudius. "Our friend must leave us, but we need not say goodbye to him, we can ask him to come back to us again some other time."

There was a howl of delight from the waiting crowds.

"Let him come back!" they shouted. "Ask him again. Get him to come to-morrow."

Claudius raised his paw for silence.

"Tawney," he cried, "on behalf of the Free Bumble-Bee people I invite you to visit us again and again."

"I'd love to," said Tawney.

"You must come," Claudius whispered; "I don't believe we have seen the last of that Black Michael and his gang. They will sneak back some day, and I know you would like to settle matters with him."

"Tawney will come again," shouted the Bees. "Hurrah for Tawney! Good old Claudius!"

"They forget their manners strangely," said Claudius sharply. "I'll trouble them to remember . . ."

At that moment there was a stir among the people, and a troop of Bees carrying an acorn-cup full of glistening liquid pushed their way forward.

"Careful," called Professor Bugloss, who was leading the party. "Take the greatest care. Be cautious. Make way for the enlarging juice."

Claudius held out his paw to Tawney.

"There is no more time left," he said; "you had better go and stand inside your clothes, then the Professor will bring the cup in through one of the sleeves. My friend: 'Until we meet again'!"

"You might say 'I'll be seeing you'!" suggested the Professor.

"Silence!" roared the Colonel. "Confound you, sir——"

Tawney stepped into the dark passage formed by the sleeve of his coat and then, turning, took the cup from the Professor's Bees who had followed him.

"Give us time to get out," said Bugloss, "then drink the mixture." He turned and ran swiftly back down the sleeve, pausing at the cuff to wave his hand.

Tawney hesitated for a moment, then raised the cup to his lips.

The sound of the Bees' band directed by Regional Harebell, playing a farewell tune, floated to him:

"Here's to the next time
And a merry meeting.
Here's to the next time . . ."

The tune faded away gently.

Tawney saw that the cloth walls round him had come closer. He felt the open collar of the shirt touch his head, then drop over on to his neck. . . .

2

Down by the pool the fish were jumping. The faint splash as one leapt for some passing fly reached Tawney's ears. He sat up, and wondered what time it was. Quite late. Why, the sun had sunk below the willow-tree, and the sky was that deep blue and red that comes only in the very late afternoon.

Tawney stood up, and then began to walk slowly towards the house.

Near the herbaceous border he met Allwood, the gardener, a pair of shears beneath his arm. They walked along together.

"I've just been finishing off clipping that top hedge," said Allwood.

Tawney nodded.

"Yes, I think I heard you," he answered.

"And don't you go forgetting to bring in that boat of yours off the pond," Allwood went on. "D'y' know, I saw a swarm of bees all over it this afternoon. Swarming, they were, on your boat, I mean. And talking of that reminds me I must come back to-night to take that wasps' nest over in the shrubbery. Those wasps are a nuisance; they stung Bill this

afternoon, and your father. He didn't half make a fuss about it. They'll sting me next—if—I don't look out. Flying about all over the place, they were. Now I don't mind those old bees—— What did you say?"

"I just said: 'I'll trouble you to remember I'm not old,'" replied Tawney.

But Allwood did not understand him.